AMERICA'S
FIRST
ELEPHANT

AMERICA'S FIRST ELEPHANT

ROBERT M. McCLUNG

ILLUSTRATED BY

MARILYN JANOVITZ

MORROW JUNIOR BOOKS/NEW YORK

To Melissa
—R. M. McC.

For my parents
—M. J.

Watercolors and color pencils were used for the full-color art. The text
type is 14 point Goudy Old Style.

Text copyright © 1991 by Robert M. McClung
Illustrations copyright © 1991 by Marilyn Janovitz
Inquiries should be addressed to
William Morrow and Company, Inc.,
1350 Avenue of the Americas,
New York, NY 10019.
Printed in Hong Kong by South China Printing Company (1988) Ltd.
1 2 3 4 5 6 7 8 9 10
Library of Congress Cataloging-in-Publication Data
McClung, Robert M.
America's first elephant / Robert M. McClung ; illustrated by
Marilyn Janovitz.
p.   cm.
Summary: Recounts how the first elephant came to America in 1795,
met President Washington, and toured the country.
ISBN 0-688-08358-7.—ISBN 0-688-08359-5 (lib. bdg.)
1. Asiatic elephant—Juvenile literature.   [1. Asiatic elephant.
2. Elephants.]   I. Janovitz, Marilyn, ill.   II. Title.
QL795.E4M43   1991
599.6′1—dc20
89-13764   CIP   AC

The *America* has brought home an elephant, from Bengal, in perfect health. It is the first ever seen in America, and is a very great curiosity. It is a female, two years old, and of the species that grows to an enormous size.

NEW YORK ARGUS, April 18, 1796

Kandi was a little Indian elephant, just two years old. She lived on the banks of the Hooghly River in Bengal, where she was being trained to be a working elephant with the Indian Forest Service.

Every morning the elephants set out for the forest, with Suri Raj, the chief keeper, riding on the back of the leading elephant. At the end of the procession came little Kandi, with Benji, the twelve-year-old son of Suri Raj, walking beside her.

Benji was small and thin. His hair was blue-black, and his eyes were the color of dark chocolate. He talked to Kandi as they walked along. Kandi waved her ears and hummed softly in reply.

All day long, while the big working elephants hauled logs through
the jungle clearings, Benji would work with Kandi. He taught her how
to kneel and lie down on command, how to pick up small logs in her
trunk, and how to raise her foreleg so he could step on it and leap onto
her back.

Every evening, when work was done, Kandi waded into the Hooghly
River with the other elephants. She splashed and rolled on the sandy
bottom and squealed with pleasure when Benji scrubbed her sides.
Then, after a good meal of hay and grain, she would fall asleep listening
to the calls of the night birds in the gathering darkness. The year was
1795.

One day that fall, a tall American with a sweeping handlebar mustache came to the Forest Service headquarters on the Hooghly River. He was Jacob Crowninshield of Salem, Massachusetts, captain of the ship *America*. He was in Calcutta to pick up cargo to take back to the United States. With him was his twelve-year-old nephew, Caleb Starbuck, the cabin boy. Caleb had tousled hair and lots of freckles.

When Caleb saw Kandi, he patted her and offered her a banana. Kandi rumbled with contentment as she stuffed it into her mouth. Then she knelt before Caleb and touched her forehead with the tip of her trunk, saluting him, as Benji had taught her to do. "She's saying thank you," Benji explained shyly.

Captain Crowninshield was delighted with Kandi's performance.

"She's a smart one!" he exclaimed. He looked long and hard at the little elephant. "It would be a great thing to bring the first elephant to America," he finally said.

Caleb nodded vigorously in agreement.

Captain Crowninshield rubbed his chin as he thought about it. Then, his mind made up, he bought Kandi. He also asked if Benji could go along to teach Caleb how to take care of Kandi. He himself would look after Benji, he told Suri Raj, and make sure that the boy got back to Bengal safe and sound after he had seen America.

When Suri Raj agreed, Benji's dark eyes sparkled. Caleb whooped with joy. The two boys looked at one another and grinned. It would be a great adventure.

The next day, Kandi trumpeted an excited good-bye to all the other elephants. Benji bade farewell to his father and mother. Then off they started, Benji on one side of Kandi and Caleb on the other side. Captain Crowninshield rode ahead on a big black horse.

The path led through the Bengal forest. Peacocks screamed from the dark shadows and jungle fowl scratched among the dry leaves. Overhead, a band of chattering monkeys swung from limb to limb of a great banyan tree and pelted Kandi with fruit. The little elephant picked up the dark red figs one by one and popped them into her mouth. Then she waved her ears in thanks.

They passed through villages where little children ran out to pet Kandi and give her pieces of sugarcane. Kandi hummed softly as she chomped them down. She loved children—and she loved to eat!

Late that afternoon, they crossed a wide bridge. Soon they were making their way through the crowded streets of Calcutta. Humped cattle wandered past them and turbaned street vendors hawked their wares.

At last they arrived at the pier where the tall-masted ship, the *America*, was docked.

Benji and Caleb tried to lead Kandi up the gangplank and onto the ship's deck, but the little elephant would not follow. She did not like the sound of the waves slapping against the pilings far below her. She refused to step on the shaky gangplank, even with Benji coaxing her with a banana and Caleb pushing.

When Captain Crowninshield saw what was happening, he ordered the crew to fasten a canvas sling around Kandi's belly. Thick ropes connected the sling to a pulley overhead, and then down to a windlass on deck. Turning the crank of the windlass, the sailors lifted the little elephant into the air. Kandi waved her legs and trumpeted in protest; but up she went, then down through the big open hatch and into the ship's dark hold.

There, Benji and Caleb removed the sling and led Kandi into a little fenced corral. On either side were bunks where the two boys and several members of the crew would sleep. The floor of the corral was covered with rice straw. A big wooden box held greens and vegetables for Kandi to eat. There was also a big bucket of water.

Kandi would be comfortable here. She gave a deep sigh, though, as she looked around. These were strange surroundings, and she was beginning to miss her elephant friends.

Benji put his arms around Kandi's trunk and Caleb patted her side. "You will soon make many new friends," Benji assured her. "You will see many new things in America," Caleb said. Kandi rumbled softly in reply.

One of the sailors had a little monkey, Mr. Jacco. He leaped onto Kandi's back and began to chatter to her. A gray parrot flew up from a bunk and landed on Kandi's head. He began to nibble at her ear.

"Welcome aboard," the parrot rasped. "My name is Pierre." Mr. Jacco then offered her a peanut. Kandi began to feel at home.

Early the next morning the *America* left port. Flying fish skittered above the waves and playful dolphins leaped through the spray across the ship's bow. Ahead, the great southern ocean sparkled green and blue.

Day after day the seas remained calm and the weather warm. Nearly every morning Kandi was hoisted up on deck to enjoy the fresh sea breezes. She learned how to keep her balance as the deck rose and fell, or tilted to one side or the other. When Caleb and Benji scrubbed her sides with salt water, she sighed with pleasure.

As they approached the coast of South Africa, the seas grew rough and the winds increased. One afternoon the clouds gathered in towering thunderheads. The sky grew dark as night. Jagged flashes of lightning flickered down from the black clouds. A great storm was brewing.

Soon rain began to fall—a few drops at first, then driving sheets of water. The *America* pitched and tossed in the giant waves.

Down in the hold, Kandi could barely stand up. Her water bucket rolled from side to side and empty casks crashed into the sailors' bunks. Kandi trumpeted with fear, even though Benji and Caleb were there.

Mr. Jacco clung to Kandi's trunk and whimpered. Pierre perched on Kandi's back, his wings spread to keep his balance. "Man the pumps!" he screamed above the roar of the storm. "Abandon ship, you swabs!"

Caleb stroked Pierre's ruffled feathers and held Mr. Jacco in his arms. He patted Kandi's side. The little elephant was very seasick now, and so was Benji. Neither of them was used to storms at sea.

"Don't worry," Caleb told them all. "My uncle will bring the ship through safely."

The storm lasted through the night, but when dawn came, the seas began to calm. By noon the sun had broken through the clouds and the winds had dwindled to a breeze. The *America* rounded Africa's southern tip the next day and headed northward through the Atlantic Ocean. Sailing on, the ship was soon in the sparkling blue waters of the Caribbean Sea.

They were on the last lap of the long voyage!

One morning four British warships sailed over the horizon. One of them sailed close to the *America*.

"Heave to!" the British captain shouted. His marines would be coming aboard, he said, to search for forbidden cargo. England and France were at war, and each suspected that the vessels of other countries might be carrying supplies that would help the enemy.

The red-coated marines scrambled up the rope ladder and onto the *America*'s deck. They began to search every hold and compartment on the ship.

What a surprise when they found Kandi! They clustered around the little elephant and patted her. They fed her pieces of hardtack. Benji showed them all of Kandi's tricks. The marines cheered when she snatched their lieutenant's cap and put it on her own head. Even the lieutenant grinned.

The marines did not find any forbidden cargo and finally rowed back to their own ship. Soon the British ships sailed away.

The *America* continued on her way northward. April arrived, and the days were warm and sunny. The long voyage was almost over. They would soon be in the United States.

One morning a long, low strip of green land appeared ahead—Long Island. On they sailed into a wide bay. Manhattan Island and the city of New York lay before them. Captain Crowninshield gave orders for Kandi to be put down in the hold, where no one could see her while the ship sailed up the Hudson River and tied up at a long wharf.

The next day the captain sold Kandi to Obadiah Owen, a big, jolly showman from Philadelphia. Mr. Owen was delighted with Kandi. He would exhibit her all over the United States. As America's first elephant, Kandi would be famous! Benji and Caleb would go along as elephant keepers. Mr. Jacco and Pierre would go, too, to keep Kandi company.

Early the next morning, Captain Crowninshield and his crew lined the rail as Kandi was hoisted up on deck. They waved to her and shouted farewell as she followed her friends off the ship. Kandi trumpeted good-bye to all of them.

New York was still asleep as they walked down a wide cobbled street called Broadway, past silent shops and taverns, past the lofty spire of Trinity Church and the Governor's House. To Kandi and Benji, New York looked very different from their native Bengal.

Dawn was just breaking as they arrived at a small building facing a tree-shaded park called Bowling Green. Mr. Owen led the way into the back room of the little house. This was where Kandi would stay.

What excitement the next day when people began coming in to see Kandi! There were giggling young ladies in hoopskirts and bonnets, and dignified merchants in frock coats and tall silk hats; young mothers with babies, nursemaids with little children, and fathers with older children. Not a one of them had ever seen an elephant before.

Kandi was on her best behavior. She liked to show off her tricks, and bowed and kneeled and lay down as Benji commanded. Then she helped him leap onto her back. Everyone laughed and clapped. They loved Kandi.

Caleb held out a bottle of strawberry-flavored drink. Kandi curled the tip of her trunk around the cork and pulled. Out it came with a loud *pop*. Next, Kandi grabbed the bottle in her trunk and poured the sweet red liquid down her throat. The audience cheered.

Now, Caleb picked up a little boy and put him on Kandi's back. He gave the boy a piece of bread. "Feed the elephant," he told him.

Grinning, the little boy held up the bread. Kandi promptly arched her trunk back over her head and took it.

A bigger boy offered Kandi a bun. After bowing a thank-you, she swallowed it. Then she sneezed. Big tears ran down her cheeks. The bun had been filled with hot red pepper!

The boy whooped with laughter. "I tricked the elephant," he shouted.

Kandi had the last laugh, though. Filling her trunk with water, she sprayed it all over the boy. That was her favorite trick for people who didn't treat her right.

Crowds of people came to see Kandi every day, and she loved all the attention she got. She was the toast of New York.

July 4, 1796, arrived. It was the twentieth anniversary of the signing of the Declaration of Independence, and what a celebration there was! Fireworks exploded and cannons boomed. At the tip of Manhattan Island, a huge hot-air balloon floated above the Battery. Brass bands and companies of blue-coated militia marched up Broadway.

Kandi led the parade, proudly waving the American flag in her trunk. Around her neck was a garland of red and white roses tied with blue ribbons. Benji, on a blue-and-gold blanket, sat on her back, with Mr. Jacco on one shoulder and Pierre on the other. Caleb, wearing a tricornered hat and beating a drum, marched beside them. It was an exciting day.

Soon after the big celebration, Kandi and her friends left New York on the evening ferry and headed for Philadelphia. Mr. Owen had a big exhibition hall ready for a special showing of the little elephant.

"We'll do most of our traveling at night," he told Benji and Caleb as they got off the ferry in New Jersey. "During the day, we'll keep Kandi out of sight in a barn or stable."

The summer dusk had faded to darkness as they started the long walk to Philadelphia. They passed fields of flax and corn, and ripening wheat that glistened white in the moonlight. Fireflies blinked all about them, and a fox barked in a nearby woods. An owl looked down at Kandi from an overhead branch. "*Who—who—who-o-o-o-o,*" it called.

The next day Kandi shared her quarters with four cows in a barn behind the Sign of the Hunt Inn near Newark. The cows stared at her with big dark eyes and tossed their heads suspiciously while she munched her hay and grain. A cat ran by, chasing a mouse. A plump red hen flew up on Kandi's back and perched beside Pierre and Mr. Jacco, clucking companionably. The little monkey chattered indignantly, but Kandi didn't mind.

When they reached Philadelphia a week later, Kandi was as popular there as she had been in New York. Every day enthusiastic crowds filled the exhibition hall on Market Street. Philadelphia was the nation's capital at that time, and George Washington, the first president of the United States, lived there. When he heard about Kandi, he announced that he would go to see her. Caleb and Benji were very excited.

On the morning of the big day, they scrubbed Kandi from trunk to tail and polished her toenails. Mr. Owen gave her a new red blanket bordered with white stars on a field of blue. Mr. Jacco got a new red jacket and cap. Pierre was taught to sing several bars of "Yankee Doodle."

Crowds had already gathered when Caleb and Benji escorted Kandi out onto Market Street. Trumpets blared as President Washington came riding up on a big white horse. On either side of him were aides mounted on prancing brown horses.

A brass band broke into a lively march as Kandi knelt before the President and saluted him, trumpeting noisily. Mr. Jacco took off his hat and waved it, while Pierre sang "Yankee Doodle" in his raspy voice.

Then Kandi bowed to President Washington and presented him with a small American flag. The great man smiled. He bowed to Kandi in turn and gave her a bag of sugar candy. The spectators cheered and stomped their feet. They whistled and threw bouquets of flowers to the two of them.

In response, Kandi waved her trunk and bowed again—this time to the audience. Then she picked up the flowers in her trunk and ate them, one by one.

America's first elephant traveled the length and breadth of the young United States during the next several years. She appeared in Boston and Salem and many other New England towns. She toured the South as well, venturing as far as Charleston, South Carolina, and Savannah, Georgia. She was usually exhibited in barns, taverns, or other public rooms, for the typical canvas circus tent did not come into use until much later. Everywhere she went, she attracted crowds of curious and enthusiastic Americans who had never seen an elephant before.

This story is based on historical fact, but is told as fiction.